WHERE WE GATHER

WE GATHER AT A JEWISH SYNAGOGUE

A Place in Our Community

by Emily Raij

PEBBLE
a capstone imprint

Pebble Explore is published by Pebble, an imprint of Capstone
1710 Roe Crest Drive, North Mankato, Minnesota 56003
capstonepub.com

Library of Congress Cataloging-in-Publication Data is available on the Library of Congress website.
ISBN: 9798875223327 (hardcover)
ISBN: 9798875223273 (paperback)
ISBN: 9798875223280 (ebook PDF)

Summary: Synagogues can be found all over the world. Each is unique and special in its own way. Readers get a glimpse into a synagogue to learn about the inside of the building, who gathers there, and what it brings to the community.

Editorial Credits
Designer: Sarah Bennett; Media Researchers: Svetlana Zhurkin and Rebekah Hubstenberger; Production Specialist: Tori Abraham

Image Credits
Alamy: eFesenko, 10; Getty Images: istock/MikeCherim, 6, Maskot, 4, 7, 13, Pascal Deloche, 15, Ray Tan, cover, Wendy Maeda/The Boston Globe, 19; Shutterstock: David Cohen 156, 11, 18, Donna Ellen Coleman, 14, Incomible, 20, kizuuuneko, design element (throughout), Mayan Nemanov, 12, 17, meunierd, 5, Opachevsky Irina, 8, quiggyt4, 9, Yuriy Chertok, 16

Printed and bound in China. 6274

Table of Contents

Words in **bold** are in the glossary.

Who Uses a Synagogue?

Judaism is a religion. It teaches that there is one God. Jews try to do good deeds. Followers of Judaism are called Jews. They have their own **customs**.

Jewish men and some women cover their heads with a fabric cap called a kippah.

A synagogue in Jerusalem, Israel

A synagogue is a holy place. Jewish people go there to pray. Many Jews celebrate holidays together. Weddings and other life events also take place there. A synagogue may also be called a temple or shul.

Rabbis are Jewish spiritual leaders. They teach about Judaism. They also help people pray.

It can take several years to become a rabbi.

Jewish children go to religious school at their synagogue. They learn prayers in the **Hebrew** language. Adults can take classes too. Leaders meet at the synagogue. They work on projects for the community.

People who pray at synagogues might use special prayer books.

Inside a Synagogue

People pray in the sanctuary. They sit on benches called pews that face the ark. That is a special cabinet. It holds the **Torah**, or Hebrew Bible. Jews read from the Torah during prayer services.

The ark that holds the Torah is the holiest place in the synagogue.

Sanctuaries often have stained glass windows and Star of David symbols.

The ark is on a raised platform called a bimah. The eternal light glows over it. It stays lit to remind Jews of God's presence.

Synagogue libraries have books on history, law, holidays, and other Jewish topics.

Some synagogues also have a smaller **chapel**. There might be a library too. Many have rooms to meet and learn. There is an office for the rabbi or other staff.

Synagogues often have space for events. People eat and dance there. Some Jews eat only **kosher** food. They can use the synagogue's kitchen or bring kosher food from home.

Sharing a meal is an act of love and holiness.

Events at a Synagogue

Jews may go to synagogue on Shabbat, the Jewish **Sabbath**. It is a day of rest. It lasts from Friday night to Saturday night. Jews pray at special services. They say blessings for wine and bread.

Covering their eyes during prayer helps people concentrate on their words.

Sharing food and drink after Shabbat creates a feeling of community.

In the sanctuary, Jews cover their heads with a kippah. They also wear a prayer shawl called a tallit. Afterward, they may eat together.

Jewish children work hard to prepare for a bar or bat mitzvah.

One special event is for Jewish children when they turn 13. It is called a bar or bat mitzvah. At mitzvah, the boy or girl reads from the Torah. They talk about what they learned. Later, there is often a celebration.

Hebrew school is usually taught on Sunday and another day during the week.

During the week, students attend religious school at synagogue. Adults go to meetings. They also take classes with the rabbi.

Where Are Synagogues?

There are synagogues all over the world. They are in big cities and small towns. Synagogues can be large or small. They can be old or new.

There are synagogues located around the world.

A Jewish family walking to synagogue in Israel

Some Jews will not drive on Shabbat or holidays. They need to live close enough to walk to synagogue.

A Community Space

A synagogue brings Jewish people together. They learn and pray. They share meals and celebrations.

Jewish people are led by the Torah and its teachings.

Children at a Yom Kippur holiday service blow horns called shofroth.

Synagogues can feel like a second home to Jewish people. Just like a family home, a synagogue is a big part of Jewish life.

Make a Tortilla Scroll

Want to roll the scroll? Here is a recipe for making a scroll that looks good enough to eat!

What You Need:

- soft taco or burrito-sized flour tortilla
- two pretzel rods
- cream cheese, softened
- licorice string

What You Do:

1. With an adult's help, cut the tortilla into a square.
2. Carefully spread cream cheese over the whole tortilla.
3. Place the pretzel rods on either side of the tortilla.
4. Roll the tortilla around the pretzel rods toward the center.
5. Tie the tortilla scroll up with the licorice string.

Glossary

chapel (CHAP-uhl)—a place set aside for worship

custom (KUHS-tuhm)—a tradition in a culture or society

Hebrew (HEE-broo)—a language used by ancient Israelites and modern-day Jewish people

Judaism (JOO-dee-i-zuhm)—a religion and culture based on a belief in one God and the teachings of a holy book called the Torah

kosher (KOH-shur)—prepared according to Jewish dietary laws

rabbi (RA-bye)—teachers of Jewish law who are usually leaders of a congregation

Sabbath (SAB-uth)—the Jewish day of rest, from sunset Friday to sunset Saturday

Torah (TOR-uh)—the law of God that makes up the first five books of the Hebrew Bible

Read More

Deutsch, Stacia. *Why We Celebrate Hanukkah: Everything to Know about Your Favorite Holiday.* Naperville, IL: Callisto Publishing, 2024.

Raij, Emily. *Jewish Festivals and Traditions.* North Mankato, MN: Capstone, 2025.

Singer, Marilyn. *Awe-some Days: Poems about the Jewish Holidays.* New York: Dial Books for Young Readers, 2022.

Internet Sites

BBC: A Visit to a Synagogue
bbc.co.uk/bitesize/topics/zqbw2hv/articles/zsdhtrd

Kiddle: Synagogue Facts for Kids
kids.kiddle.co/Synagogue

Synagogues360
synagogues-360.anumuseum.org.il/about-us

Index

About the Author

Emily Raij has written more than 40 books for children and edited dozens of professional resources for K-12 teachers. She is a native of Chicago, where she earned her journalism degree from Northwestern University. She lives in Florida with her husband, daughter, son, and dog.

WHERE WE GATHER

WE GATHER AT A HINDU MANDIR

A Place in Our Community

by Lisa J. Amstutz

PEBBLE
a capstone imprint

Published by Pebble, an imprint of Capstone
1710 Roe Crest Drive, North Mankato, Minnesota 56003
capstonepub.com

Library of Congress Cataloging-in-Publication Data
Names: Amstutz, Lisa J., author.
Title: We gather at a Hindu mandir : a place in our community / by Lisa J. Amstutz.
Description: North Mankato, Minnesota : Pebble, an imprint of Capstone, [2026] | Series: Where we gather | Includes bibliographical references and index. | Audience: Ages 5-8 | Audience: Grades 2-3 | Summary: "Hindu mandirs are places of worship. People who follow the Hindu way of life gather to pray and celebrate. Some mandirs are small and simple. Others are large and elaborate. People enter through a gate or a tower. Shrines line the walls. Mandirs are places of peace and places to learn. An activity is included to help kids extend their learning"— Provided by publisher.
Identifiers: LCCN 2024054913 (print) | LCCN 2024054914 (ebook) | ISBN 9798875223082 (hardcover) | ISBN 9798875223037 (paperback) | ISBN 9798875223044 (pdf) | ISBN 9798875223051 (epub) | ISBN 9798875223068 (kindle edition)
Subjects: LCSH: Hindu temples—Juvenile literature.
Classification: LCC BL1243.74 .A525 2026 (print) | LCC BL1243.74 (ebook) | DDC 294.5/35—dc23/eng/20250113
LC record available at https://lccn.loc.gov/2024054913
LC ebook record available at https://lccn.loc.gov/2024054914

Editorial Credits
Designer: Sarah Bennett; Media Researcher: Rebekah Hubstenberger; Production Specialist: Tori Abraham

Consultant Credits
Devala Rees, Educational Researcher, Hindu American Foundation

Image Credits
Alamy: Cavan Images/Thomas L. Kelly/Aurora Photos, 17; Getty Images: benedek, 16, hadynyah, 9, iStock/GorazdBertalanic, 7, iStock/Krishna Narendra, 19, Mayur Kakade, 14, Oli Scarff, 6, oversnap, 8, Philippe Lissac, 13, Rob Stothard, 4, 5; Shutterstock: Anton Starikov, 20 (paper), Dinesh Hukmani, 15, kizuuuneko, design element (throughout), Krysja, 18, Leonid Andronov, cover, Photo Spirit, 10, pjhpix, 11, reddees, 12, Sarah2, 20 (craft sticks)

APPROVED BY
HINDU AMERICAN FOUNDATION

Printed and bound in China. 6274

Table of Contents

Words in **bold** are in the glossary.

What Is a Mandir?

The Hindu **religion** is 4,000 years old. People who practice Hinduism visit temples called mandirs. They are usually quiet and peaceful places. But during festivals, they can be loud!

People gather at a mandir in England.

Lights symbolize knowledge and power.

A mandir is a home for **deities**. Leaders called priests may live nearby. People come to the mandir to worship and pray. They celebrate holidays and enjoy music and art. They learn about the Hindu faith.

A temple in London, England

A mandir can be big or small. It may look like a home or like a palace.

Some mandirs have tall domes and gateways. They have many carvings of flowers, deities, and spirits. The buildings are often **symmetrical**.

The Pura Bratan is a temple that worships the deity Shiva.

The door faces east to let in morning sunlight. A flag shows which main deity the temple serves. There are often gardens and water nearby.

Look Inside!

People enter the mandir through a gate or tower. Shoes are left at the door. Wearing nice clothes is a form of respect.

People in colorful clothing enter a mandir in India.

Ringing bells clear the mind.

People may bow or touch the ground when they enter. They bring gifts such as fruit or flowers. They ring bells to focus before prayer.

Inside is the prayer hall. A row of **shrines** lines the walls. Inside each shrine is a deity. The statue or image is called a **murti**. People stop and show respect at each shrine.

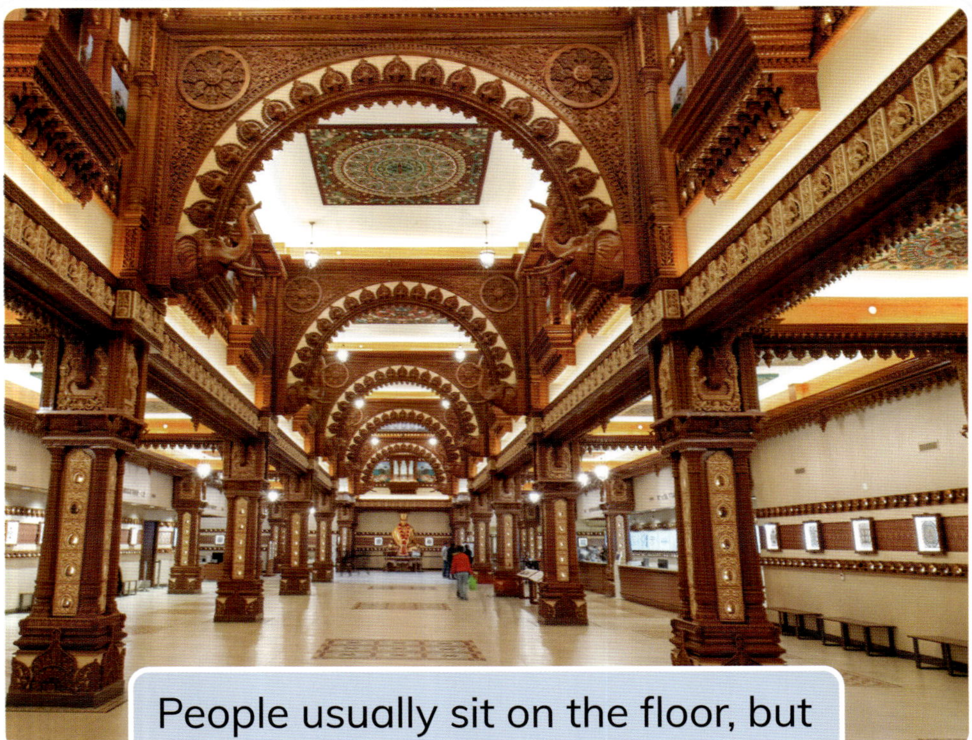

People usually sit on the floor, but benches are also available.

Priests wash and dress the murtis. They put flowers and fruit on the shrines. An **altar** holds very special murtis.

Some temples have shrines just for women.

Several times each day, a priest performs a ceremony called **puja**. The ceremony shows respect to the gods. People may chant along or participate silently.

A temple priest in India performs puja and chants prayers.

Offerings show respect to deities.

Flowers and food are offered to the gods. People also give **incense**, water, and a lamp. It is believed that the deity enjoys the food and water. By tasting it, they have blessed it. People share the food later.

Who Worships Here?

There are more than 1 billion Hindus living around the world. Many live in India. But they are found on every continent.

Almost all Hindu homes have a small mandir.

Community members are invited to attend Hindu festivals.

Hinduism is a way of life. Brahman is the life force. The deities are different forms of Brahman.

Reaching Out

Mandirs are used for more than prayer. They are meeting places. People learn yoga together. There are classes to learn Hindu traditions. Some mandirs host music and dance programs or art shows.

Weekly Hindu classes for children are called Bala Vihar.

People gather at a mandir.

A mandir is a place to celebrate. People come for Hindu holidays. They honor weddings and important life events.

Mandirs often help those in need. They may offer clothing or shelter. Some have community kitchens. They serve meals to anyone who is hungry. The Tirupati Temple in India serves 100,000 people a day!

Food is offered to the gods. Then it is shared by people in the temple.

The Tirupati Temple in India is the most popular mandir in the world.

Is there a mandir near you? It may offer tours. Maybe you can stop by for a visit!

Make a Model Mandir

What You Need:

- construction paper or card stock
- glue
- scissors
- craft sticks
- markers or crayons
- modeling clay

What You Do:

1. Look at some pictures of mandirs.
2. Build a model mandir using paper, glue, scissors, and craft sticks.
3. Use markers or crayons and the modeling clay to decorate the mandir.

Glossary

altar (AWL-tuhr)—a table or platform used for religious rituals

deity (DEE-uh-tee)—a god or goddess

incense (IN-sens)—sticks that make a sweet smell when they are burned

murti (MUHR-tee)—the image of a deity

puja (POO-jah)—Hindu worship

religion (ri-LIJ-uhn)—a set of spiritual practices and beliefs that people follow

shrine (SHRINE)—a place used for religious worship

symmetrical (si-MET-ruh-kuhl)—the same on both sides of a center line

Read More

Andrews, Elizabeth. *Hindu Mythology*. Minneapolis: Pop!, a division of ABDO, 2025.

Ganeri, Anita. *Hindu Festivals and Traditions*. North Mankato, MN: Capstone, 2025.

Ramkumar, Ranjeeta. *Holi*. North Mankato, MN: Capstone, 2024.

Internet Sites

BBC: A Visit to a Mandir
bbc.co.uk/bitesize/articles/z8c22v4

Hinduism: Sacred Spaces and Places
uri.org/kids/world-religions/hindu-spaces

Kiddle: Mandir Facts for Kids
kids.kiddle.co/Mandir

Index

About the Author

Lisa J. Amstutz is the author of more than 150 children's books on topics ranging from applesauce to zebra mussels. An ecologist by training, she enjoys sharing her love of nature with kids. Lisa lives on a small farm with her family.